In honor of Ed Carriere

Suquamish History

Co-Salish waters and land

To the cedar tree, seed to basket

Published by Oh Little Cedar Basket
Address all inquiries to:
Ila Barlean
(206) 465-4430
ilabarlean@gmail.com
www.OhLittleCedarBasket.com

ISBN: 979-8-99-26322-0-0
Library of Congress Control Number: 2025903676

Illustrator: Anne Peters
Editor: Tyler Tichelaar, Superior Book Productions
Cover Design & Interior Book Layout: Seattle Printworks

Every attempt has been made to properly source all quotes.

Printed in the United States of America

First Edition

2 4 6 8 10 12

Oh Little Cedar Basket

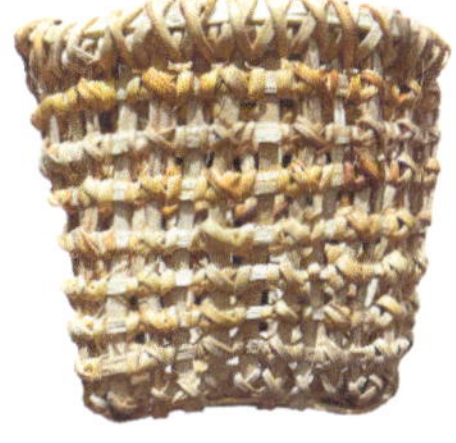

Ila Barlean

Illustrator Anne Peters

"The tree which moves some to tears of joy,

is in the eyes of others only a green thing

which stands in the way. As a man is, so he sees."

— William Blake, English poet and painter (1757-1827)

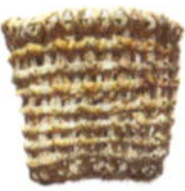

Oh, Great Cedar Tree, how grateful I am to thee.

You grow from a little seed in the rich
warm dark earth of our land.

And with the love of the sun, grow into a strong
tall cedar tree, with strong, long-reaching roots.

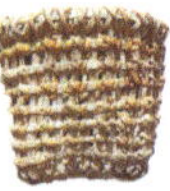

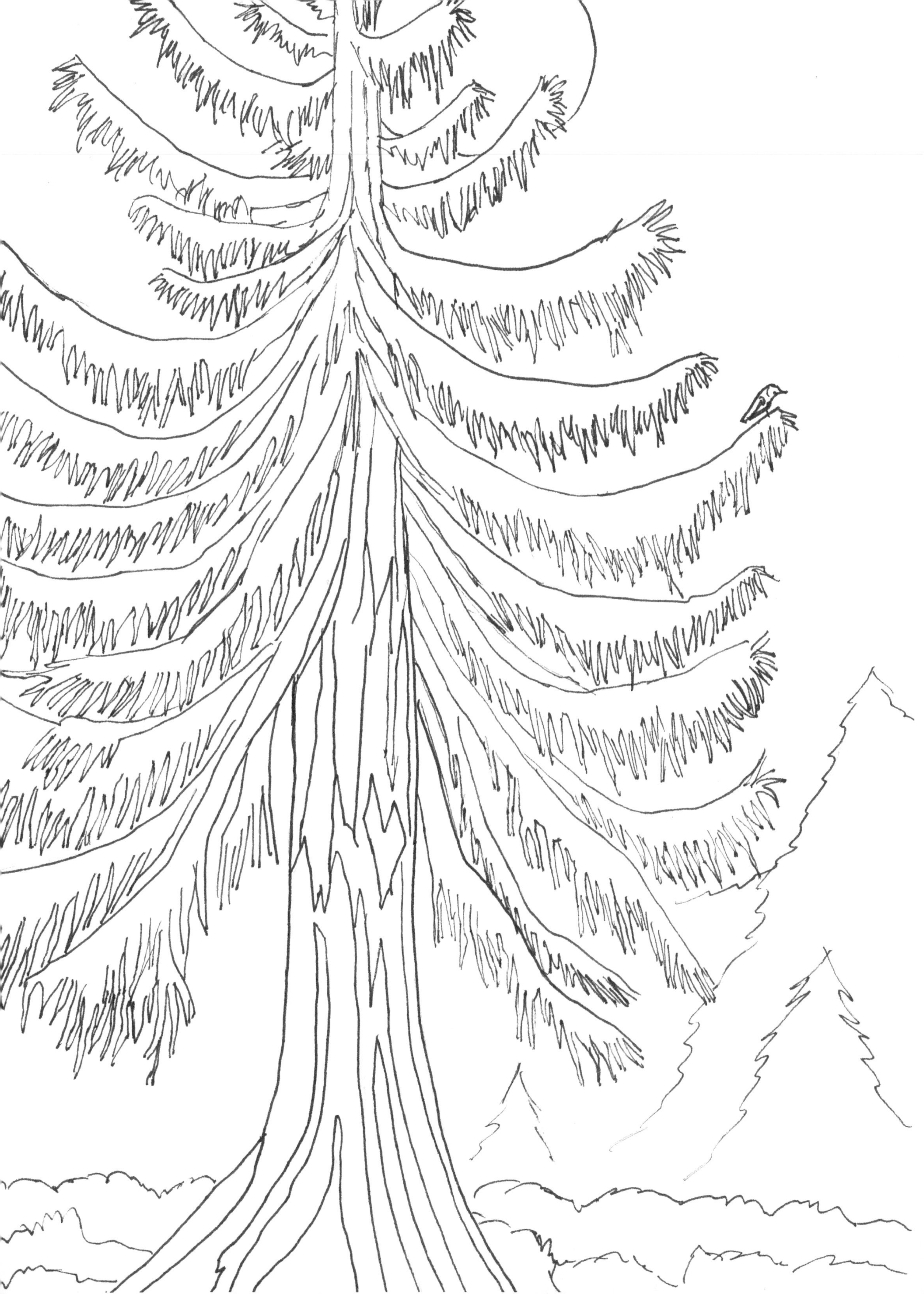

Oh, great cedar tree, how grateful I am to thee.

Your bark makes my clothes.

Your seeds heal my soul.

Your limbs and roots make my baskets.

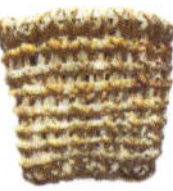

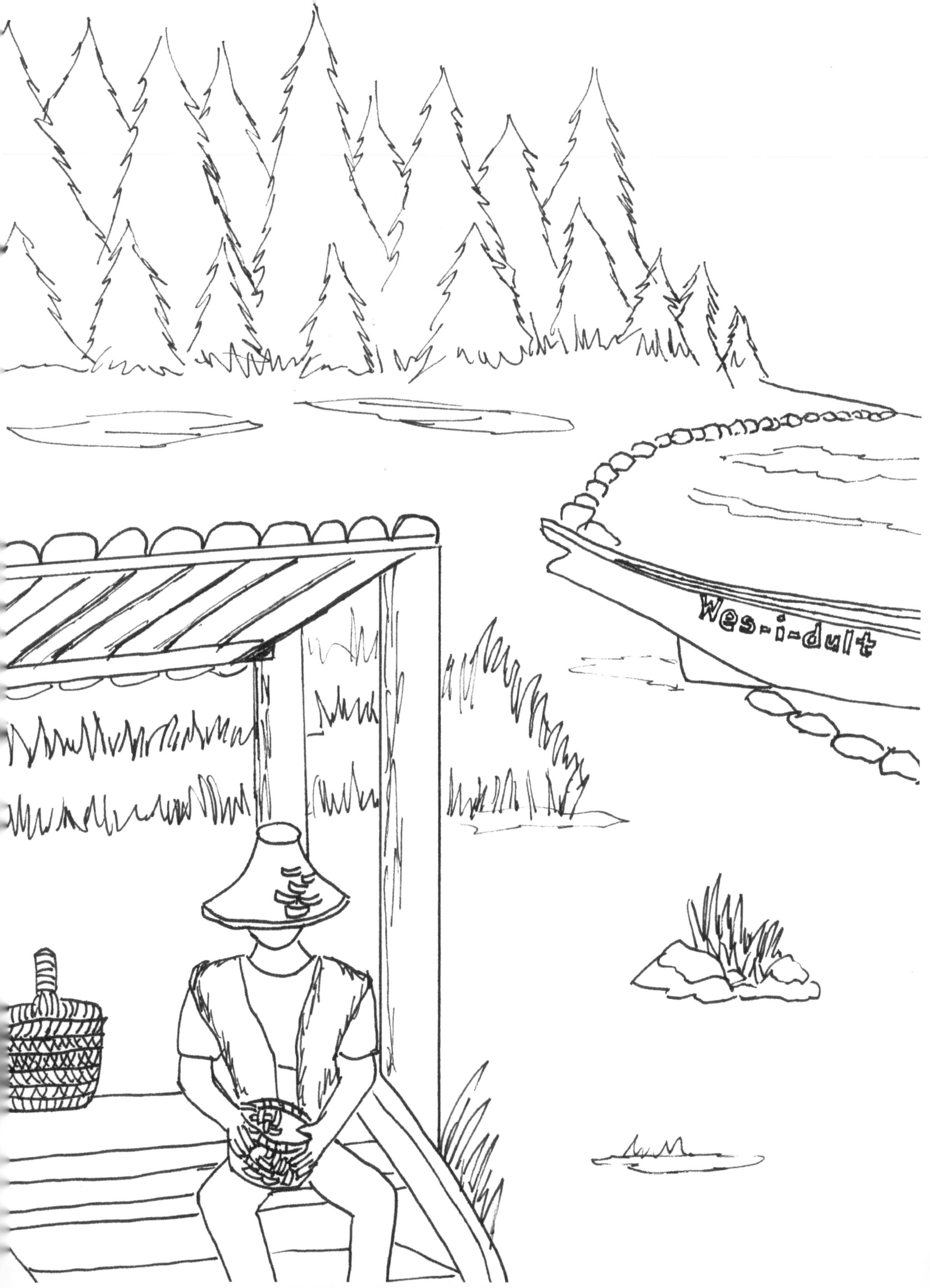

Wes-i-dult

Oh, great cedar tree, how grateful I am to thee.

Each basket helps me on my way
with each coming day.

One basket for cooking,

One basket for berries,

One basket for clams,

One basket for salmon,

One basket for my child,

One basket to tell this story.

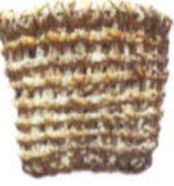

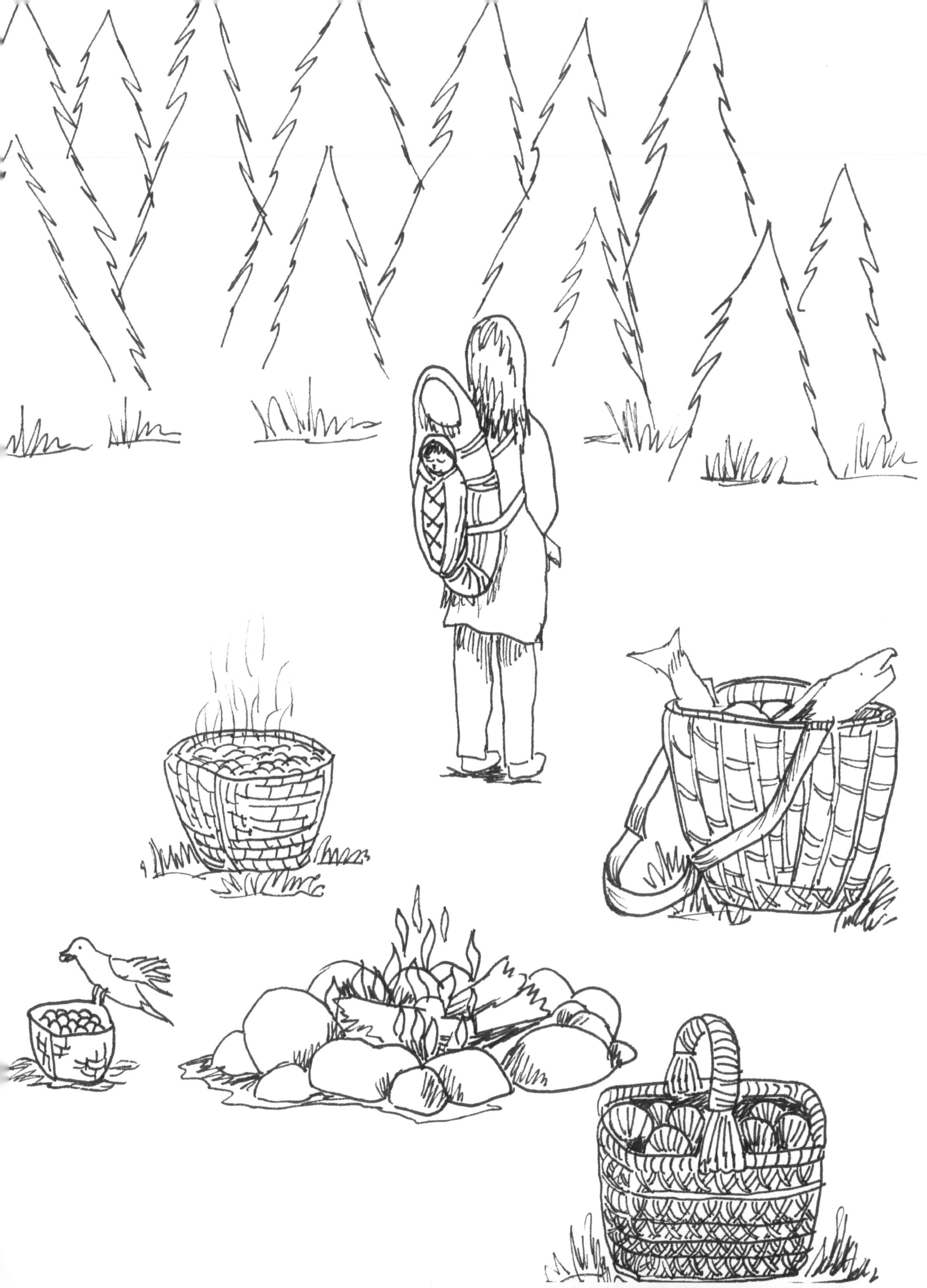

Oh, great cedar tree, how grateful I am to thee.

When a great strong wind brought you to the ground, we come to your side so you can carry on.

We pause to pray for your sacrifice to give us life. Then we gather all of you. Your roots. Your limbs. Your bark. Your body. Your seeds. For soon you will be more than just a little cedar basket.

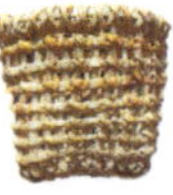

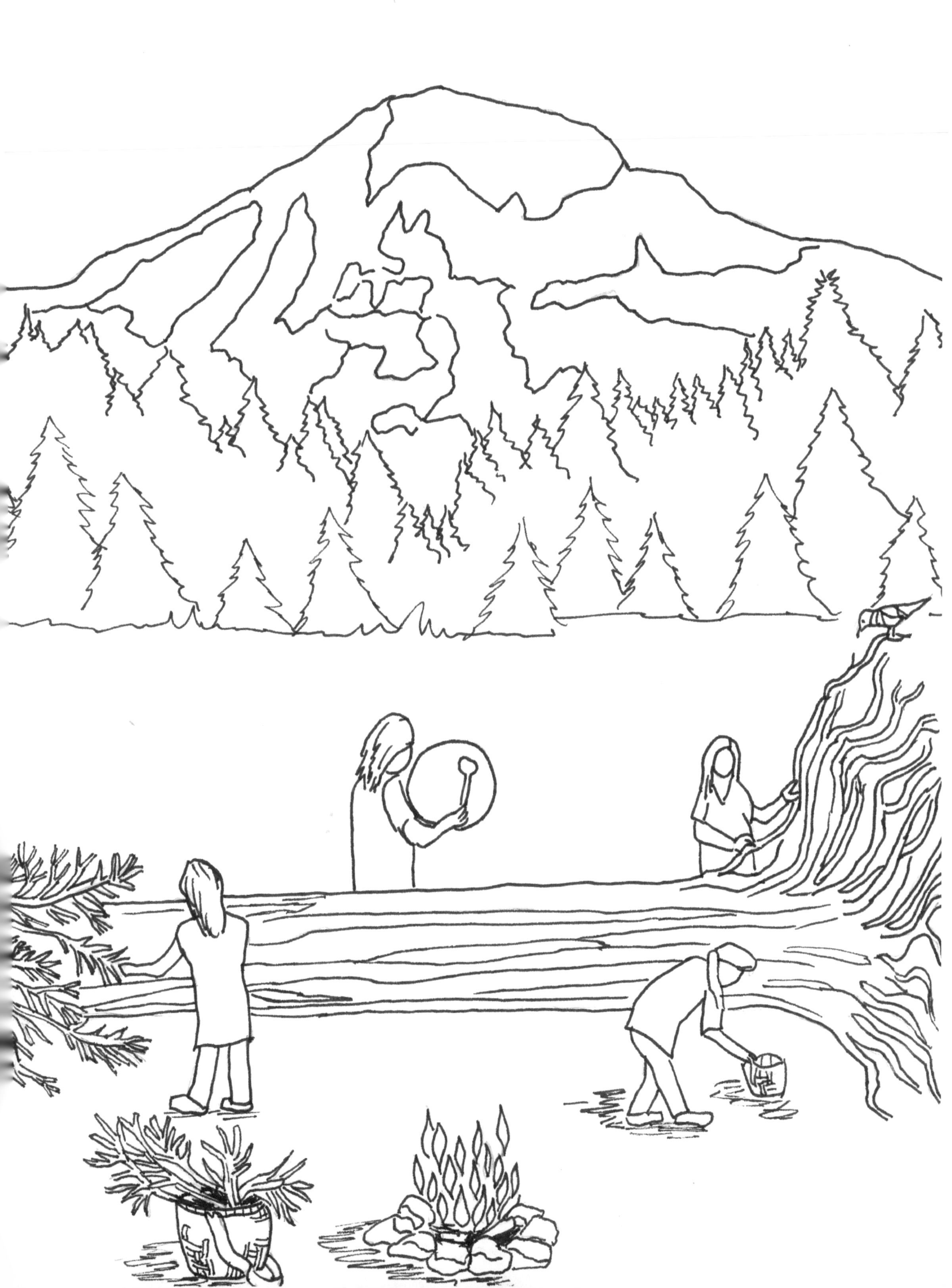

Oh, great cedar tree, how grateful I am to thee.

My elder has said, "It's time to make a basket."

This is the way of our peoples.

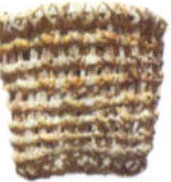

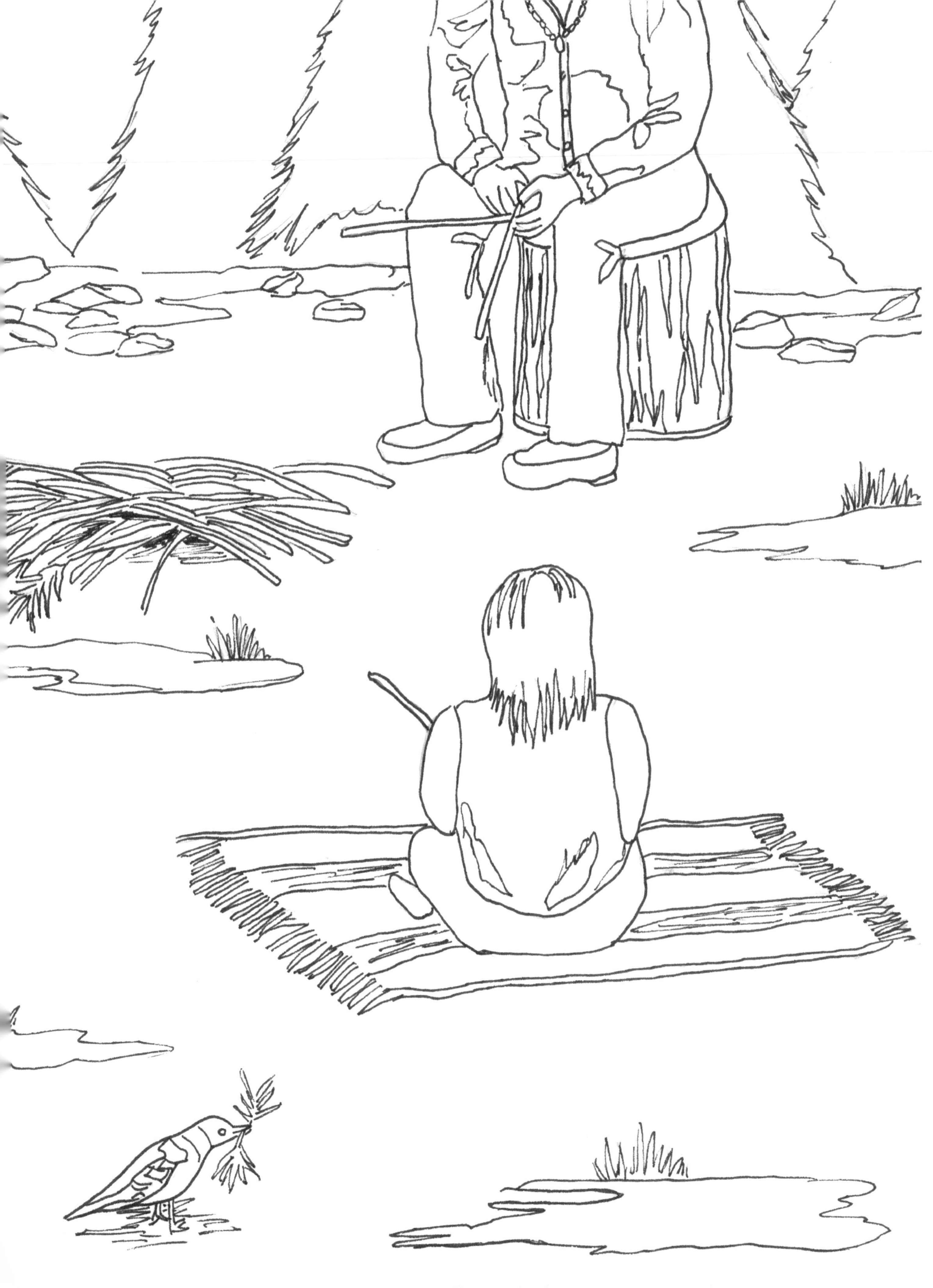

Oh, great cedar tree, how grateful I am to thee.

We clean and prepare your gathered roots
and trimmed limbs and peel your beautiful
protective bark.

As we separate your limbs from one to two, we soon
discover you have a soft side and a strong side.

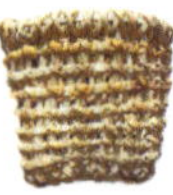

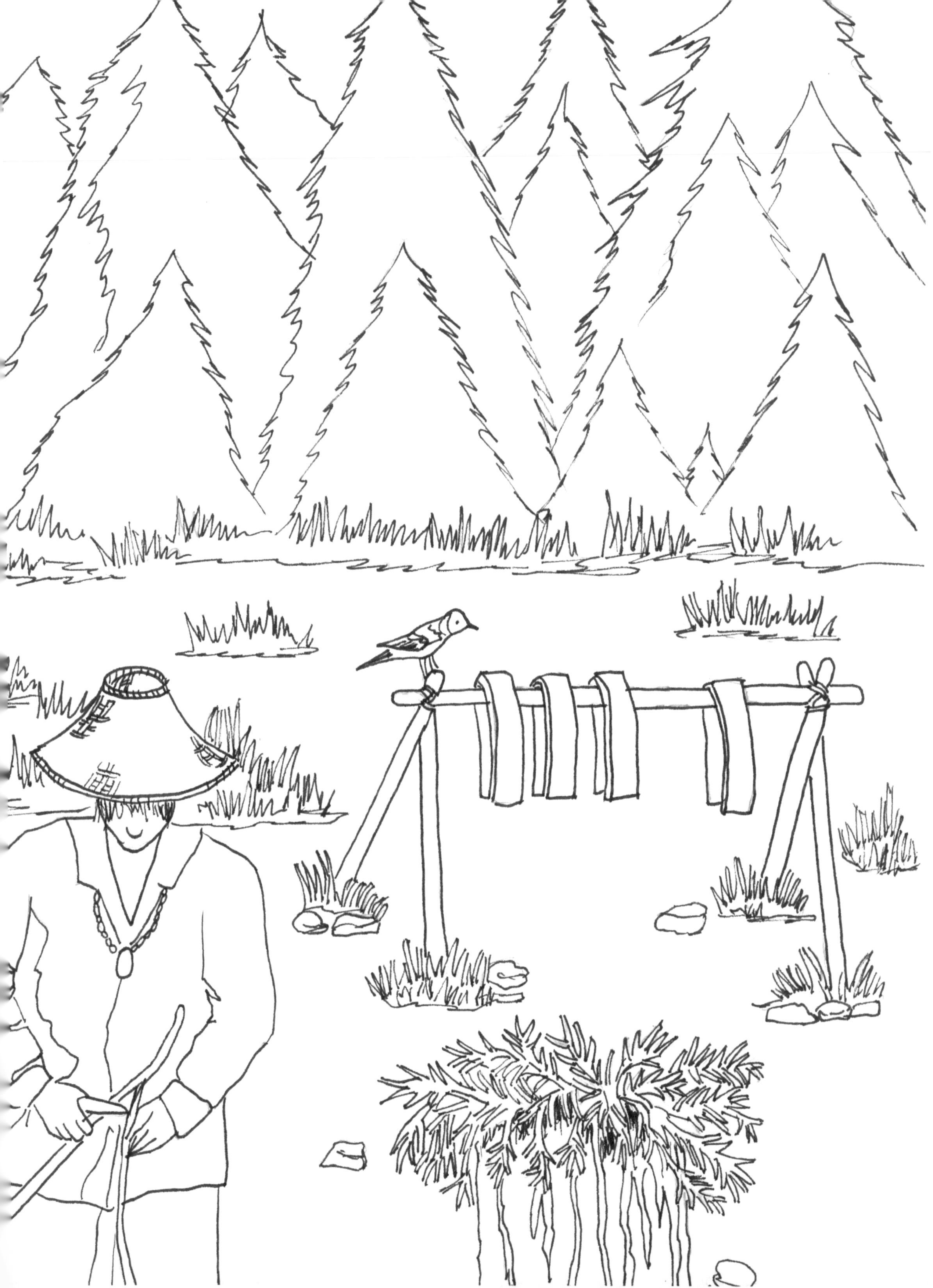

Oh, great cedar tree, how grateful I am to thee.

Your strong side of the limb is of great sturdy strength, and soon, we learn you will be the puller guiding, yet hardly seen.

Your soft side of the limb is so strong and flexible that we soon discover you will be the warp, creating the body of the little cedar basket.

And your long-reaching, mighty roots are so strong and so flexible that we learned very quickly your roots want to be the weavers of the little cedar basket. For, just like when your roots were in the ground, they like to reach all around.

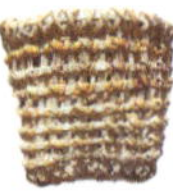

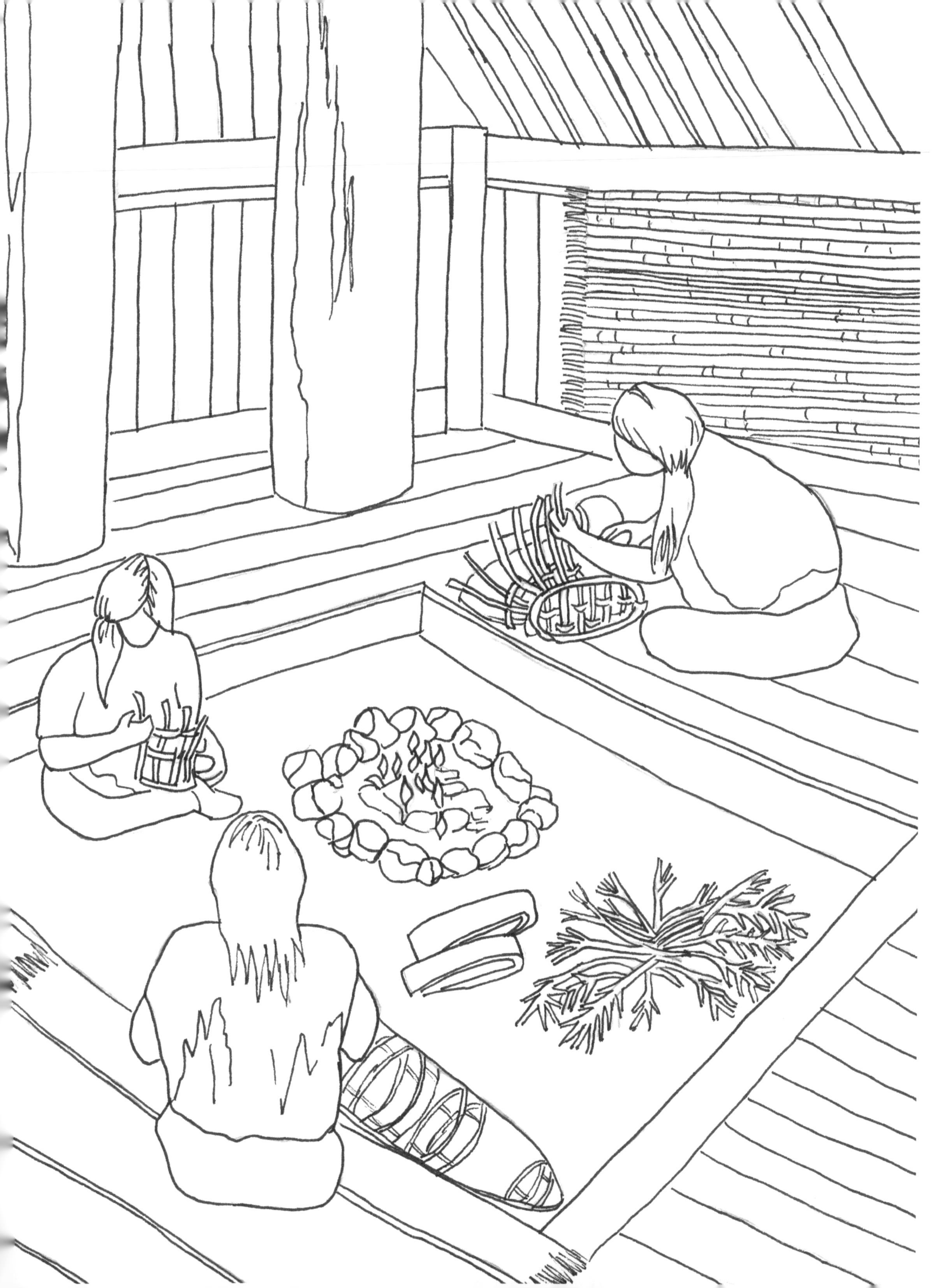

Oh, great cedar tree, how grateful I am to thee.

Just like the place where you were born.

We create a beautiful pattern for the foundation
of the little cedar basket.

In order to grow, it's best that we have a
good teaching to start life.

Such as our mother and father guiding us each
day and night in delight.

Oh, great cedar tree, your roots of wisdom weave
in the locker weave for your foundation needs
to be stable and true.

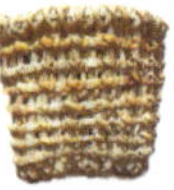

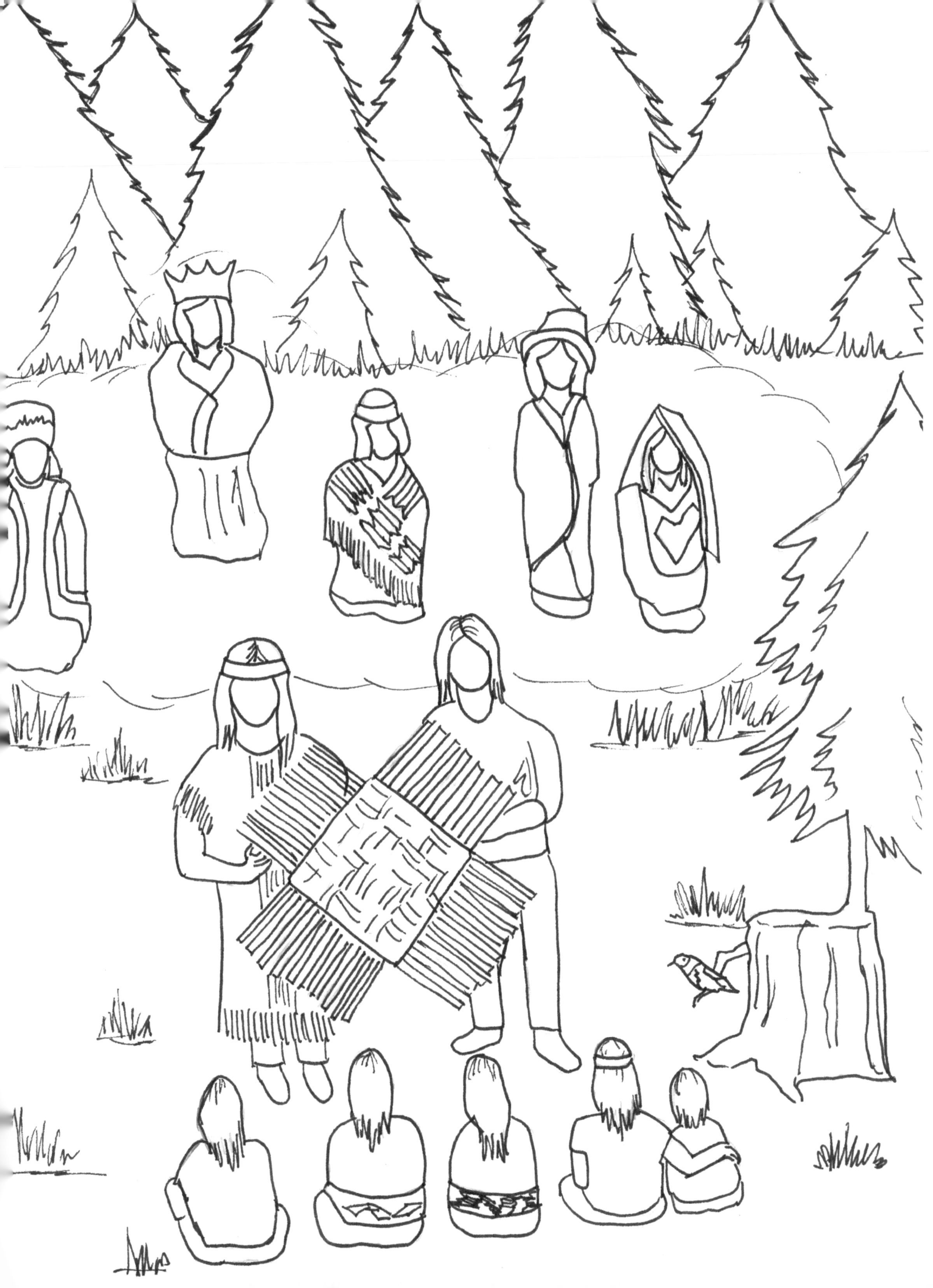

Oh, great cedar tree, how grateful I am to thee.

Like the path of life that we travel meeting
each lesson along the way, we next set in
the puller to guide the weaver along the
warps of the little cedar basket.

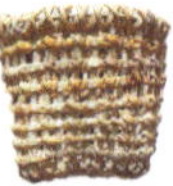

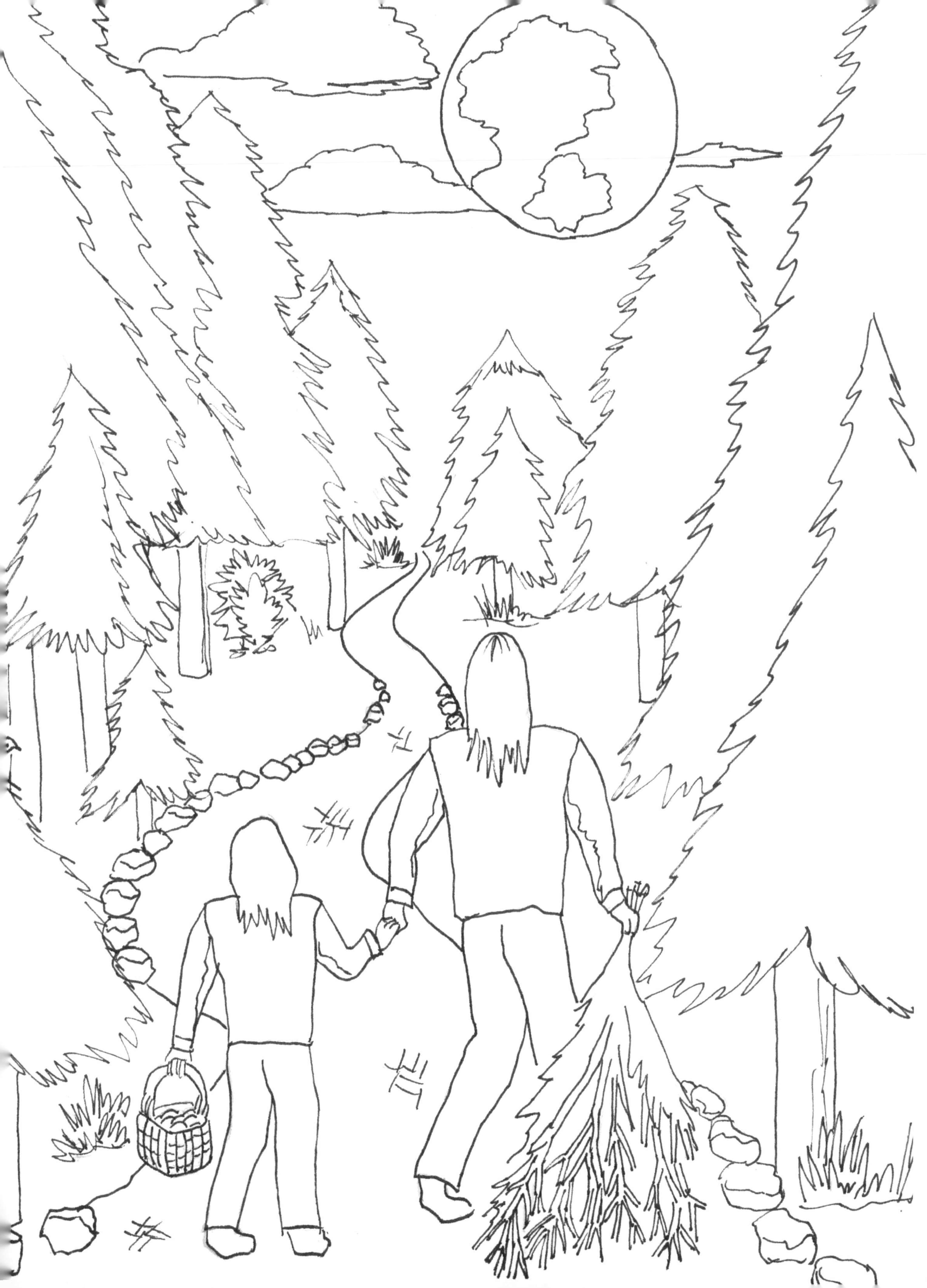

Oh, great cedar tree, how grateful I am to thee.

You teach me to be mindful.

You teach me to be free.

You teach me to be patient.

You teach me to be me.

Each bend, wrap, and fold tells
a story not yet told.

Oh, great cedar tree, your roots and limbs dance
in me, creating this little cedar basket.

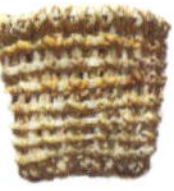

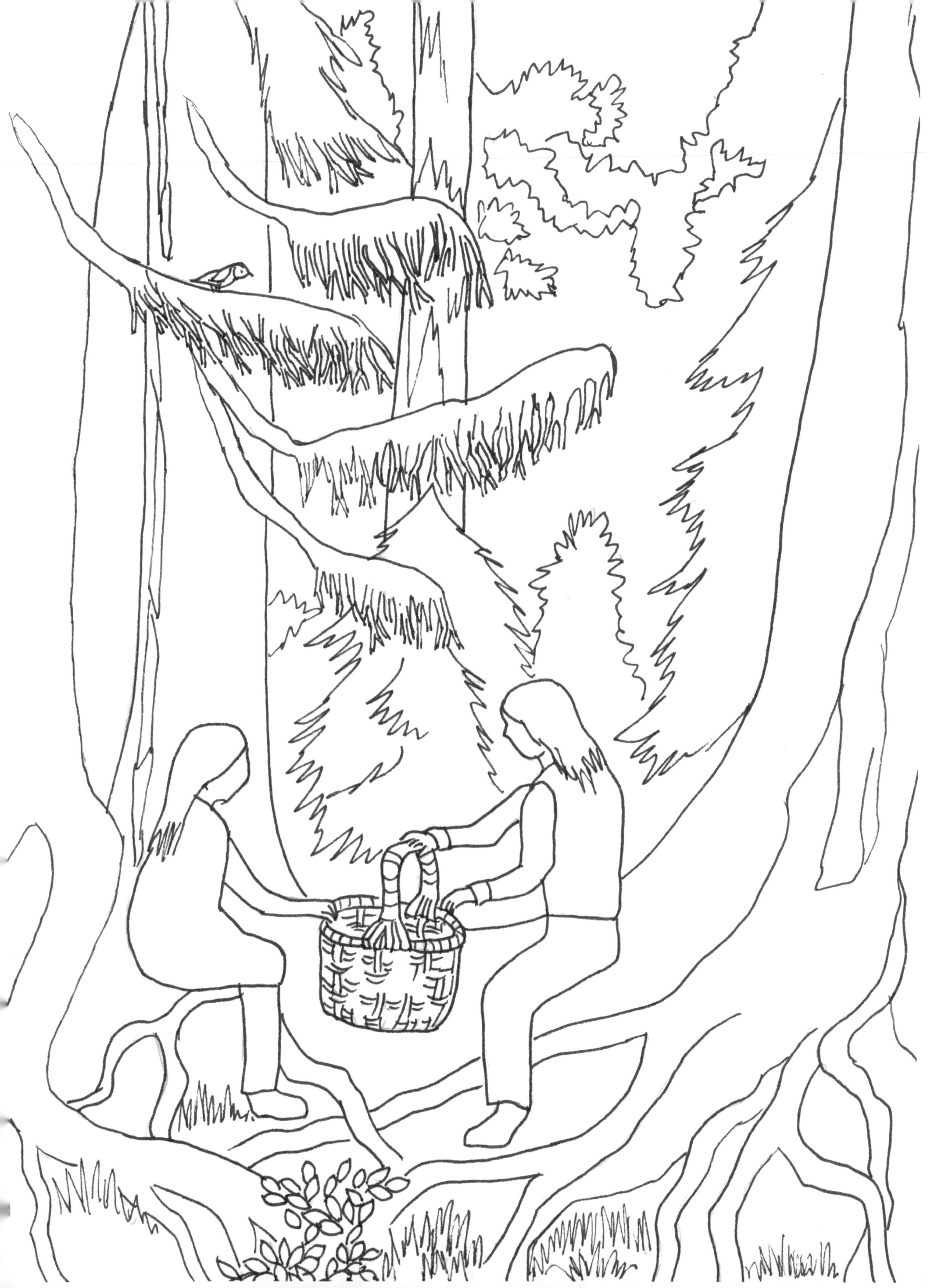

Oh, great cedar tree, how grateful I am to thee.

We feel, push, and pull for the basket is not far.

Around and around your body we go.
Like the earth around the sun,
we travel together as one.

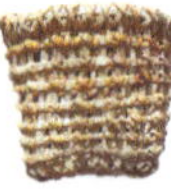

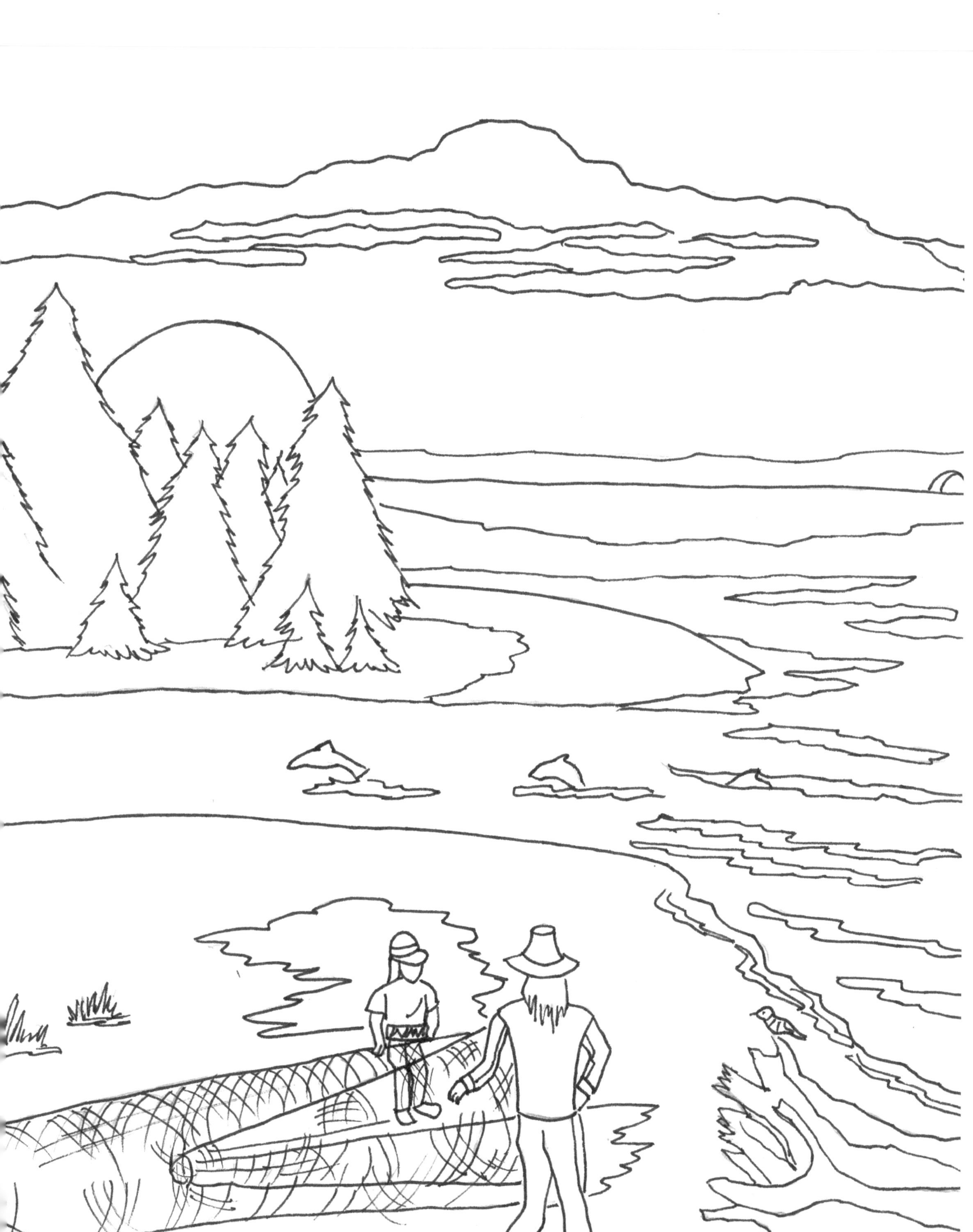

Oh, great cedar tree, how grateful I am to thee.

Like each night when we shut off the light.
Oh, little cedar basket, we need to make you tight.

Creating your brim with a smooth bend and fold.
We have journeyed together, and your story
will forever unfold.

It's time for life to carry on.

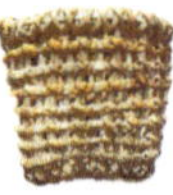

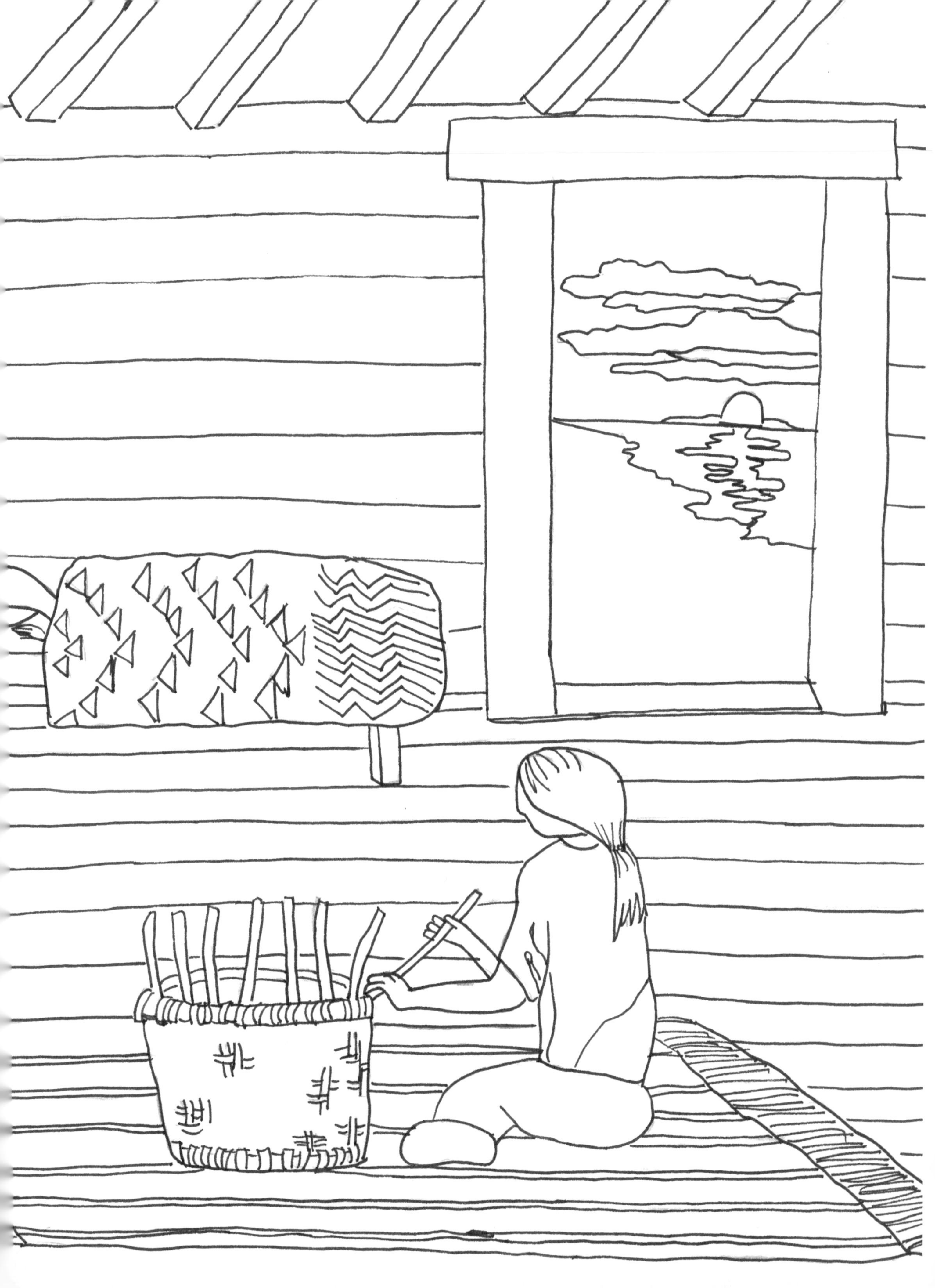

Oh, little cedar basket, how grateful I am to thee.

We have journeyed together thus far,
and now here you are!

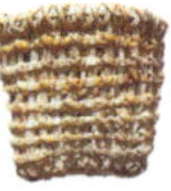

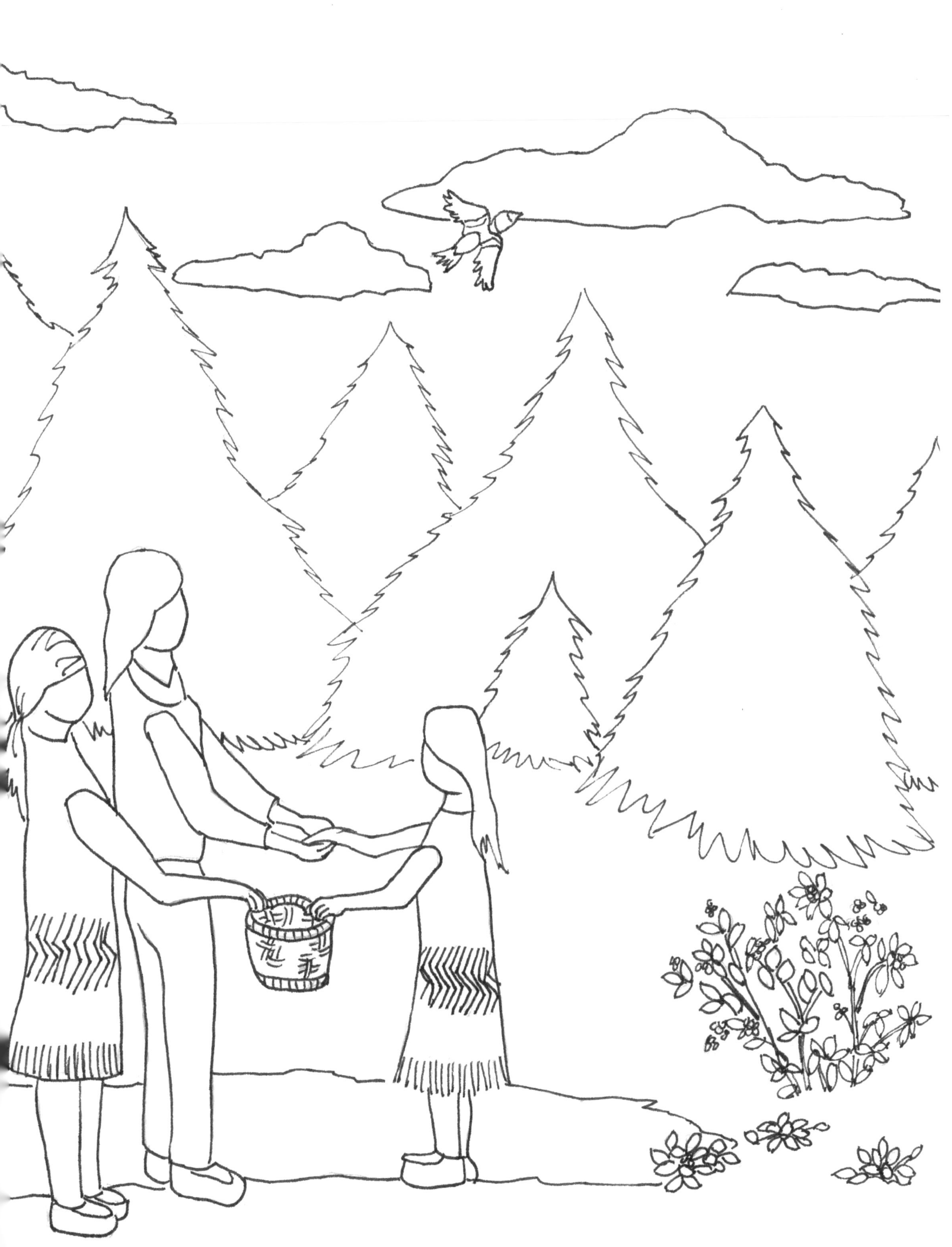

About the Western Tanager Bird

As a spirit animal, the western tanager symbolizes joy, hope, and new beginnings. In the Pacific Northwest and Coast Salish waters, it can be seen in the spring and warm summer months when the sap of the cedar tree is warming up and starts to flow from the roots to the limbs.

With the tanagers bright plumage, beautiful song voice, this colorful little bird has been a symbol of joyous beginnings while bringing peace and inner joy to many souls.

Coming out of the cold winter months this little bird, with its bright colorful plumage, brings new hope with the spring and warm summer months that follow.

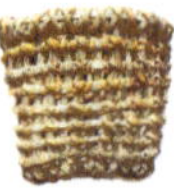

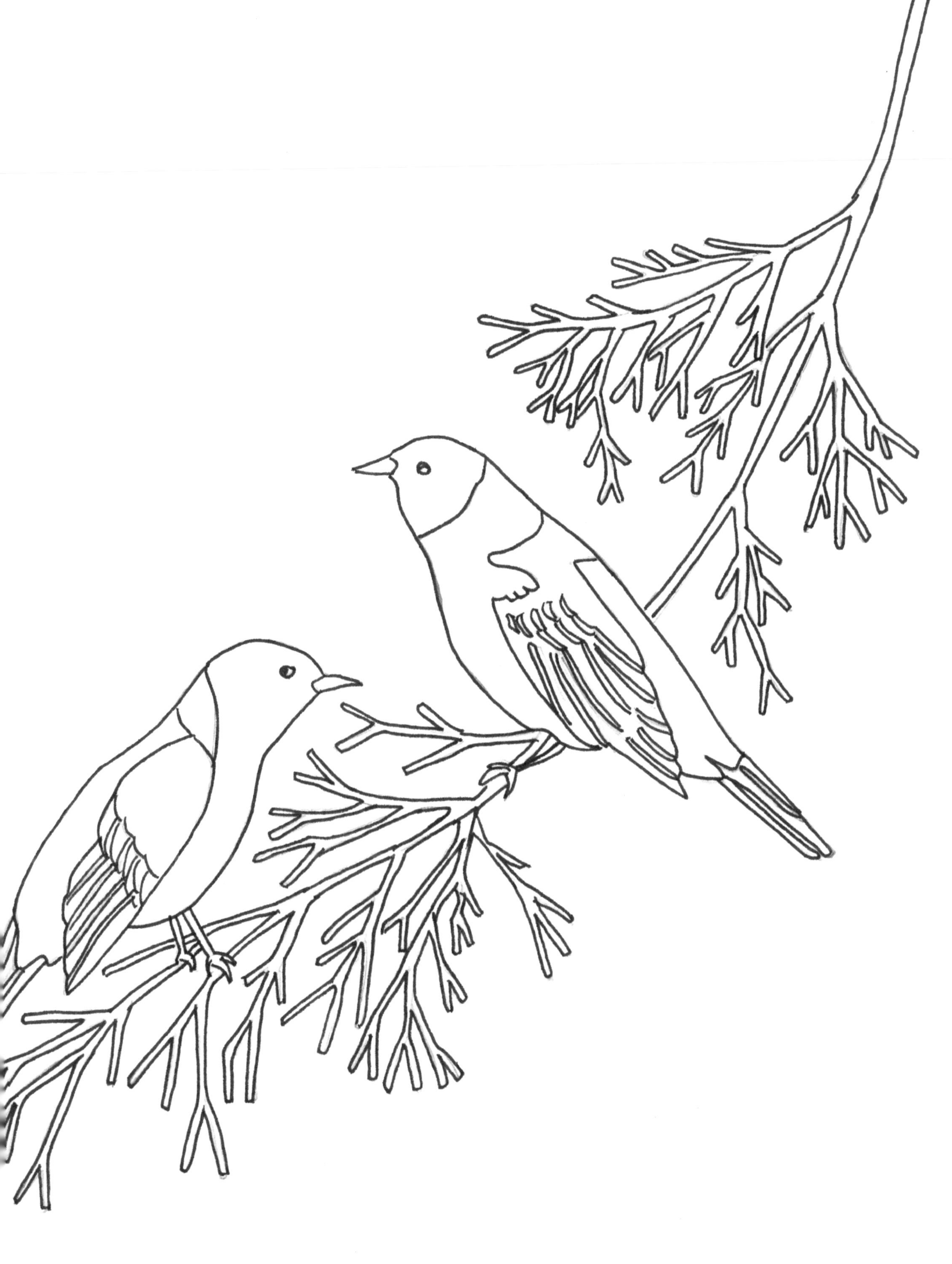

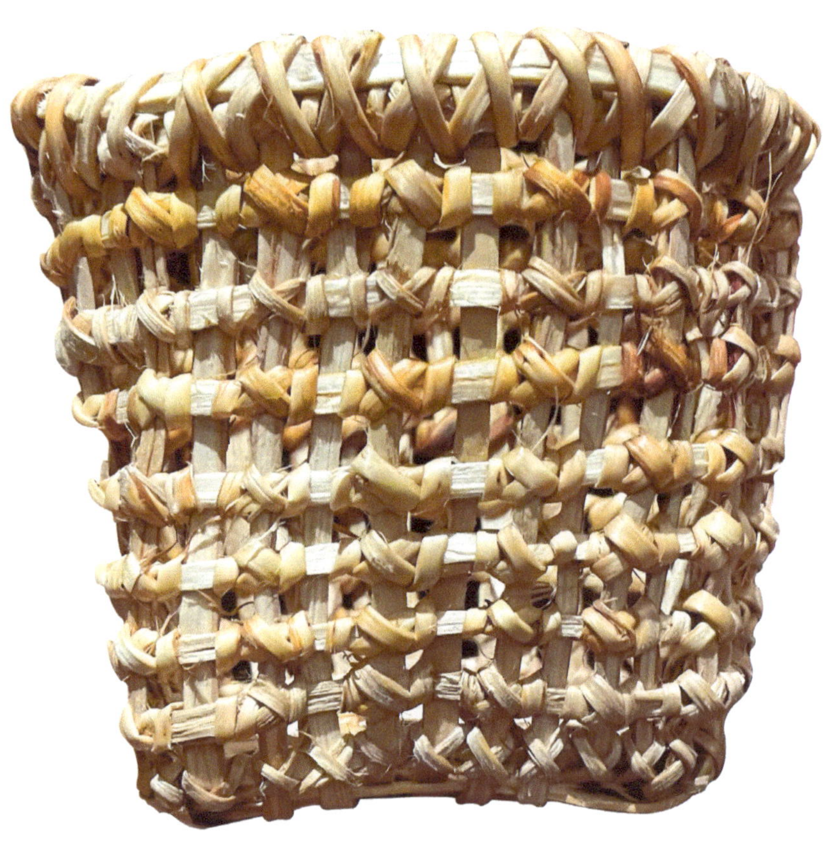

Glossary

Brim: The top edge or rim of the basket. A fold-and-wind weave, folding the edges of the warp to the inside of the basket and wrapping the warp with a weaver, creating a bundle on the inside of the basket.

Locker Weave: Once the bottom of the basket is made, then you go around the outside edges of the basket and do a locker weave to those edges. Once the locker weave is set, the basket will stay in place. The choices of locker weave are a two-strand twining weave or a cross-warp weave.

Puller: A straight piece running around the inside of the basket, used when weaving a cross-warp weave or a reverse-stitch weave.

Warp: The vertical fibers that form the body of the basket.

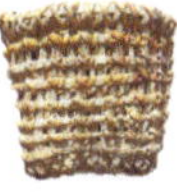

Meet the Artists Whose Work Inspired This Book

About the Author

Ila Barlean hails from the Pacific Northwest. In 2014, she had the opportunity to meet Master Weaver, Ed Carriere, a Suquamish Elder and recipient of the 2023 National Endowment for the Arts Fellowship for keeping alive the tradition of making the Coast Salish Clam Basket. Since meeting Ed, Ila's relationship with the cedar tree, the basket, and Coast Salish weaving has strengthened under his wisdom and guidance. Ila is honored to share her inspired experience in this little book. May it inspire respect and remembrance that Native Cultures are alive here.

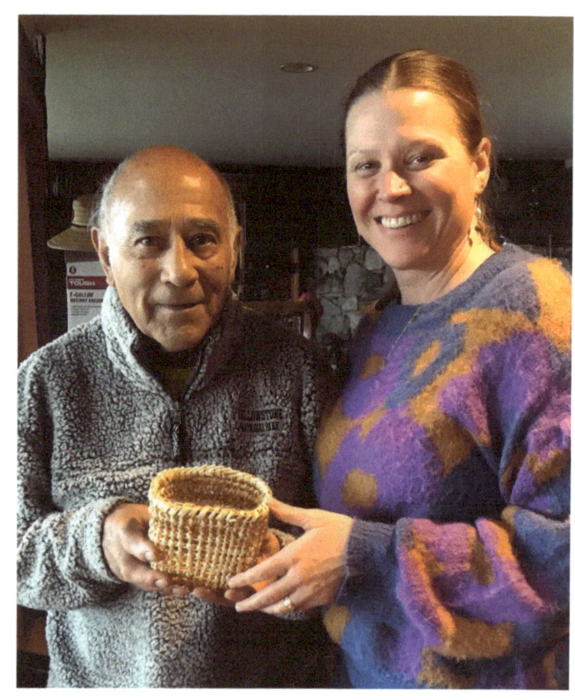

About Ed Carriere

Ed Carriere is a native to the Suquamish Coast Salish Tribe and has been living on trust land since 1934. He has spent a lifetime respecting and honoring his elders and family blood line by keeping native basketry alive. Among the many books and awards for which Ed has been recognized, in 2022, he received the First Peoples Fund Community Spirit Award. He can be found on his 80 acres of trust land in his home weaving with cedar limb, cedar roots, stinging nettle, spruce root, tuli, cattail, and many more fibers of the land.

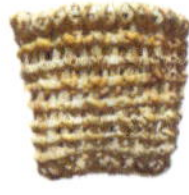

About Danielle Morsette

Danielle Morsette is a Coast Salish artist from the Suquamish Tribe and Stó:lō Nation (Shxwhá:y Village) residing on the Port Madison Indian Reservation in Washington State. Danielle's artistic journey began in 2003. Her weaving is done entirely by hand on a traditional loom with minimal tools, producing garments for ceremonial and celebratory purposes, as well as weavings for public display. Ila has been inspired by how Danielle's work is infused with respect for the mathematical precision inherent in Coast Salish design.

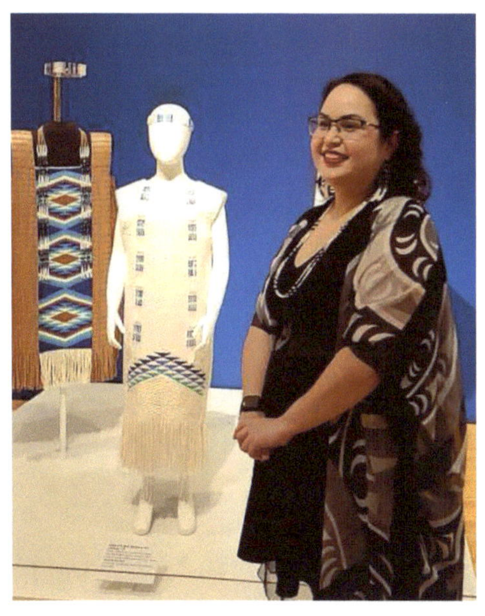

About the Illustrator

Anne Peters lives in Kitsap County, Washington. She is a graduate of the Northwest College of Arts and Design. Anne's art magically captures the natural beauty of landscapes, seascapes, wildlife, and much more, employing colored pencil, oils, acrylics, and airbrush to create her beautiful art.

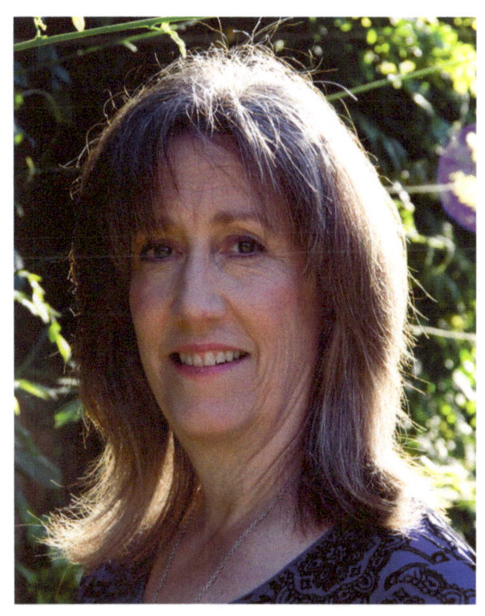

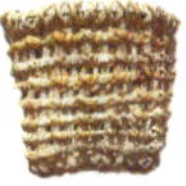